The Misadventures of Belle & Chloe

A book of short stories about two insane chocolate Labs growing up in Texas.

By Doyle Walker

Copyright © 2011 by Doyle R. Walker
The author can be reached at:
doyle@belleandchloe.com

All rights reserved. No part of this book may be used or reproduced in any manner whatsoever without written permission, except in the case of brief quotations embodied in critical articles and reviews. For information contact Wild Icon Publishing Group at info@wildicon.com.

Walker, Doyle.
The Misadventures of Belle & Chloe: a book of short stories about two insane chocolate Labs growing up in Texas / by Doyle Walker.
p. cm.
Includes index.
Second Printing

SUMMARY: These twenty short stories recount the adventures of two chocolate labs, sisters Belle and Chloe. The tales, many told by the more assertive dog, Belle, describe their fun with squirrels, ducks, and backyard Texas cookouts, from the time they were weaned until the present.

Audience: All ages, but especially grades 4-9
978-0-9799335-4-7 ISBN 13
0-9799335-4-7 ISBN 10

1. Labrador retriever–Juvenile fiction. 2. Labrador retriever–Fiction.
3. Dogs–Fiction.   I. Title.   II. Title: Misadventures of Belle and Chloe.

PZ7.W15235Mis 2009   [Fic]
QBI08-600347

Printed and bound in the United States of America

Published in the United States by:
Wild Icon Publishing Group
www.WildIcon.com
Info@WildIcon.com

This book is dedicated to my grandson,
Jake Reed Walker

May you grow up realizing that dogs may not be our whole life, But they certainly make our lives whole.

And also to my wife
Cathy,

Who certainly makes my life whole.

Acknowledgements

I never could have written this book by myself, and I am most appreciative to all my friends and colleagues who provided me with so much positive influence along the way. You are too numerous to mention, but I thank each and every one of you.

There are, of course, some people I simply can't leave out. I must first express my love and gratitude for the support and encouragement given to me by my wife, Cathy, without whom this book might have never reached fruition. After all, it was because of her that I wrote it in the first place. She loved the idea of stories involving our lovable Labs, and she believed in my ability to write them even before I did myself.

I also want to thank my son and daughter-in-law, Chris and Kamryn, for all the hours of enjoyment their two little yapper dogs, Molly and Coconut, continue to give Belle and Chloe. When they come for a visit, Belle of course tries to ignore her little hyper cousins, while Chloe welcomes both of them into our house with open paws. Also, prior to this book going to press, our kids gave us our first grandchild. I can only imagine the many stories involving Jake, Belle and Chloe that lie in the near future, and the addition of Molly and Coco to the mix will only provide multitudes more.

I owe a huge debt of gratitude to each of the following for providing something special to the making of this book. Thanks must go to Belle and Chloe's veterinarians, Dr. Terry Lee, D.V.M. and Dr. Andrea Swinson, D.V.M., along with their entire hospital staff, for maintaining our dogs' health all these years. Credit also goes to my friend Todd Friedman, of the Wild Icon Publishing Group, for literally taking me by the hand and teaching me the 'ins-and-outs' of publishing. I am sure that without his advice and coaching, many of my stories would still be languishing in my laptop. Thanks also to my friend and Jostens colleague, Jim Bellomo, for his 'website wizardry'. The ideas Jim had while creating my belleandchloe.com site were simply amazing. I am also grateful to the family of Johnny and Fran Balsamo, for not only being wonderful friends, but for encouraging me to "quit talking about it and publish the thing, for Pete's sake!" Their enthusiasm meant more to me than they will ever know. Thanks also go to Ralph Trimmer and Jonathan Upchurch for initially helping me get this project up and running from almost day one. My heartfelt thanks also go to Lisette Cunningham for her contagious humor, as well as her amazing artistic and graphic talents, and to three amazing ladies: Pat Futch, Jill Hotz, and Brandy Schaefer...not only for their superior copyediting skills, but for their friendship as well.

And finally, thank you to Dr. John's Sal and Sadie...for reminding everyone they ever met that no one can fully understand the meaning of love...until he has owned a dog. I wish Belle and Chloe could have met you guys. You would have been great pals.

Contents

    Introduction: My Name's Belle, and My Sister is Chloe .... *vii*

1. Love at First Sight *1*
2. Why I Don't Walk the Dogs *4*
3. Rusty and the Rat *8*
4. Chloe and the Ducks *15*
5. Molly and Coconut *19*
6. Belle Has a Lump *22*
7. Molly and the Possum *25*
8. The Den Just Isn't Big Enough for Two Labs and a Squirrel *30*
9. Mouth-to-Snout Resuscitation *35*
10. Giving Your Dog CPR *41*
11. Chloe and the Door-to-Door Preachers *44*
12. How to Beg...A Lab's Point of View *48*
13. There's a Squirrel in the Flowerbed (and powdered dog pee, too) *53*
14. Top 10 Ways I Know I'm Owned by a Chocolate Lab *59*
15. Belle and Chloe's Memorial Day Picnic *62*
16. Looking at Christmas Lights *65*
17. There's a New, Pink Addition to the Family *70*
18. The Mister and the Bassinette *73*
19. We're Going to the Parade...I think! *79*
20. Doing What We Do Best *83*

    Afterword: Why the Mister Wrote This Book *86*

    Index *88*

Ralph Trimmer

Introduction:
My Name's Belle, and My Sister is Chloe

Hi folks. My name's Belle, and I'm what they call a chocolate Labrador retriever. That's pretty much a mouthful of words that makes me sound kind of fancy, but really I'm just a dog that does dog things. Oh, and I kind of look like a big ol' tootsie roll, which is something I've discovered really tastes good and is about the chewiest thing I've ever come across in all my dog years, but the Mister gets really, really mad if he ever catches me eating one. I've got a sister named Chloe...more about her later...and together we live in this big, brick dog house with the Mister and the Missus.

I pretty much run things around here. When I was a pup, I was called the "Alpha Dog" by the vet...I don't know what she meant by that, but I'll tell you this about her: she may be good at making me feel better when I'm kind of puny, but she also has things that she can pull out of nowhere that pokes me and sticks me and brother let me tell you that she can hide something called a thermometer where things just shouldn't be hidden. But like I said, she knows how to make me and my sister feel better when we really feel lousy, and she's a good ear scratcher, too. Anyway, as I was sayin', I'm the leader around here although I let the Missus think she runs things, just like she kind of lets the Mister think he's the boss around here. But

anyone who knows anything knows that Belle Walker rules the roost. And Chloe pretty much falls in line, 'cause she "doesn't want to hurt anyone's feelings", for Pete's sake. She just does as she's told, which I totally don't understand, but I gotta admit, it does make life easier for me around here.

Well, I hope you like this here dog book, and I'm sure you will. Why? Because it's filled with stories about me and Chloe, of course. And if it wasn't for us, this here brick dog house would be about the dullest and quietest place in the world to live. But we're what the Missus calls "Lovable", and what the Mister calls "his little Headaches". I don't really know what either means, but when the Missus talks about us she's always smilin', which is more than I can say for the Mister. But they don't know what they'd do without us, and actually, we don't know what we'd do without them...we just never tell 'em that, though. Chloe and I like to keep 'em on their toes, if you know what I mean and I'm sure you do.

Now go curl up in a nice quiet corner and read this here book. You're gonna enjoy it.

Love at First Sight

I figure there's no one better to explain how Belle and Chloe became part of our household than me...the "Mister" in these stories.

How does one pick out puppies from a large litter of Labs? And how can one be sure that the pups you're planning on taking home...pups that will become members of the family and will live with you for years and years to come... how can one be sure they'll fit in? Can one trust "love at first sight"? And how in the world does one select the right names?

Here's the story of how Belle and Chloe became Belle and Chloe Walker...

Memorial Day weekend, 2000, was truly special for the Walker household. Our son graduated from The University of Texas on Saturday, and on Monday my wife Cathy and I brought home two of the cutest little chocolate Labs you would ever see.

A friend of ours had a female Labrador retriever named Cheyenne, and she had given birth to a litter of Lab pups in April. By the time Memorial Day rolled around, the two that we had picked out were ready to come home.

But how do you choose the correct pup? And not one pup, but two? When they were about six weeks old, we visited Cheyenne and sat on the ground and watched her pups interact. One of them immediately ran over to me and started tugging on my tennis shoe laces. I would pick her up, hand her to Cathy, and immediately she would run back over and attack my shoes like she was Attila the Lab. She was the perfect little alpha female. Now, while my laces were being eaten, another little pup was hiding behind some ivy growing up the patio wall. Little Attila ran over to her sister and started biting and playing tug-of-war with her tail. Well, the little shy one eventually got tired of having her tail chewed on, and she let out a ferocious bark...OK, at six weeks of age, it was more like a ferocious squeak...but Attila got the point and quickly let go. So Cathy and I figured the little shy one not only must be Attila's favorite playmate, but she could hold her own in a tussle. So that's how we selected our two pups.

For the next month, while the pups remained with Cheyenne to finish weaning, Cathy and I looked through every baby name book we could find (for some reason, Cathy didn't think "Attila" was a proper name for a little girl, even a little girl who thought she was boss). And how did we finally settle on their names? Cathy chose them from the names of two characters on her favorite Soap Opera, "Days of Our Lives". The two names selected were: Belle and Chloe, with Belle being the alpha female and Chloe being her shy, tug-of-war buddy.

On Memorial Day, we drove over to pick up the newest members of our family. On the way home we stopped by our vet for a "puppy check-up", got the all-clear sign, and took them home. How on earth would we have ever known that these two little angels would develop two such distinct personalities in the months to come. Belle, the dominant female, became Cathy's shadow, always being by her side and commanding the respect of any dog within range, while Chloe, the shy one, became the mischievous, lovable little soul who followed me everywhere I went.

Between the two of them, our lives would never be the same.

Why I Don't Walk the Dogs

As the Mister in this family, I've always enjoyed watching my neighbors walk their dogs. There's just something very peaceful about the act. The trusting relationship that exists between a dog and his master is a time-honored tradition in a civilized land, and observing the animal as it obediently heels, stays, and comes on command can be very impressive indeed. So as soon as Belle and Chloe learned to walk on a leash, I decided that it was time for the three of us to join the nightly neighborhood parade.

One would think that it would be an extremely easy process to hook a leash to a dog's collar. And if you had tiny little yapper dogs, or even large normal dogs, I suppose it would

be. But Belle and Chloe are not normal dogs. Belle is a bit easier to handle, but only because she has a touch of arthritis which helps slow her down. So when she thinks she's jumping up and down, it's actually her head bobbing around and the rest of her body just kind of waddling right and left. If you can catch her head and hold it still, you can hook the leash.

But then there's Chloe. She makes Belle look like she's in a coma. Chloe doesn't run like a normal dog. She bounces from point A to point B...as if she has pogo sticks for legs. And while she's bouncing all over the backyard, she's smiling constantly. And when she has this huge grin on her face, her tongue takes on a life of its own (and of course, with her 5 pound tongue comes a gallon or two of slobber).

After about twenty minutes of attempting to hook their leashes onto their collars, I finally give up and tackle each dog, pull their collars up and over their heads and then, while holding each collar in my scraped and bloody hands, connect the leashes. I then tackle them again, shove their collars back over their heads and lo and behold...we're ready to take our leisurely and restful walk...after I crawl over to the patio and sit down and rest for about ten minutes.

As the three of us exit the backyard, two of us...and I'm assuming you can guess which two...try to see who can run out the gate first. Belle is always used to being first in everything, and Chloe just does things spontaneously,

without ever thinking. Now, a pair of chocolate Labrador retrievers are about 4 feet wide standing shoulder to shoulder, and the gate seems to be about 3 feet, 11 inches from post to post. And when the two dogs try to get out of the gate at the same time, it's like pounding a round peg into a square hole. It just doesn't go. And neither do they. So I'm pulling on Chloe's leash while using my size 13 tennis shoe to coax Belle's butt through the gate and out the backyard. Once Belle's out, Chloe easily bounces out right behind her, slobbering as if it's monsoon season. So after about 45 minutes, we're good to go.

Now, to get from the backyard to the front sidewalk, we must walk through our side yard...between our house and neighbor Bill's. And to make this 50 foot trek, we must pass a host of shrubs, vines, flowers, three bird feeders, a squirrel feeder, and one cat named Rusty sitting inside neighbor Bill's kitchen window. This short walk takes at least another ten minutes, because each dog has to sniff, scratch, taste, and mark her territory just about every step of the way. Until they reach Bill's kitchen window, that is. It was at that

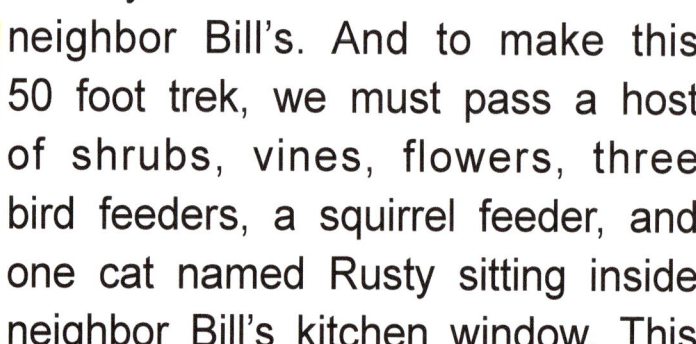

very moment that I decided perhaps these dogs simply weren't ready to visit the great outdoors.

Belle saw Rusty first, and in her inquisitive nature she decided to walk up to the window and check things out, nose to nose. Of course, to walk up to the kitchen window required knocking over a 50 pound marble bird bath like it was made of plastic, and trampling Bill's azalea bushes. As I yanked and pulled on her leash, Chloe spotted the feline and made a beeline to and almost through the window. She didn't trample the azaleas, because she literally bounced over them. Instead, she hit the kitchen window about waist high (do dogs even have waists?) and with her tongue practically sticking to the glass, scared the bejeebers out of the cat. Rusty then leapt from the window sill, landed on Bill's kitchen counter, knocked over his blender, toaster and can opener, bounced off the microwave and then shot like a Chinese rocket through the den in a blur of cat hair and fur balls. I immediately dropped their leashes, scooped the dogs up in my arms and, together with the hernia they just gave me carried them into the backyard, where I deposited them in a dog pile. I then crawled across the patio, staggered into our den, locked the back door, and turned off all the lights.

If anyone ever tries to walk those dogs again, it'll be Cathy. I'll be the one staying home with the doors locked and the blinds closed.

Rusty and the Rat

Hi folks...Chloe here, and I'm finally going to get to tell one of these stories. Now my sister Belle seems to think she's the only one around this place that can tell stories. Why she thinks this I don't know, but I've been told by my other dog buddies that I can tell stories just as good as my sister. It's just that she won't let anybody else ever get a word in edgewise. I mean, once she starts talkin', she just won't stop. So I'm guessing that in order to constantly talk, it must require a lot of hot air.

And everyone in our neighborhood knows that Belle Walker is so full of hot air it pretty much comes out of both ends, if you know what I mean and I'm pretty sure you do. Not only can that dog talk circles around one of them door-to-door preachers that I discuss later in this book, but she can clear a room when that hot air escapes out of places that should only be used for dog introductions. I mean to tell you that the biggest surprise us dogs can have is when we walk up to one another to sniff our hellos and receive a blast of something that can make your whiskers fall out. But I digress. That's not what this tale is all about, so to speak. Instead, it's about our neighbor Bill's cat, Rusty, and his encounter with the neighborhood rat.

They've been buildin' new houses all around our neighborhood, and what used to be big, open pastures is now turning into brand new homes. And because these new homes are takin' up space where a bunch of critters used to live...like rabbits and birds and stuff...well, these critters are now movin' into our territory. Now, Belle and I can take care of them rabbits and birds and squirrels and possums and things. They're not a problem at all. Heck, if the truth be known, I'm friends with this cottontail that lives down the alley. He comes by every so often and eats a few of the Missus' flowers, and then he and I just

lay in the sun and he tells me what it's like on the other side of the fence. He's a nice bunny, as for as rabbits go, but there's one critter neither Belle nor I care too much for, and that's Mr. Rat.

You see, rats kind of keep to themselves. They like to prowl around at night and eat bugs and worms and other things that just shouldn't be eaten. And as long as they stay out of the Mister's house, well, me and Belle really don't care much to mess with 'em. I mean, you never know where they've been, and you sure don't know what they've been in, if you know what I mean. So, we let Rusty take care of the rat population. And why? Well, because that's just what cats do. I mean... that's their job. In fact, I can't think of any other reason cats are here, other than to control them rodents. I mean, what good are they otherwise? If they're not lickin' and cleanin' themselves, then they're hackin' up fur balls and making a mess on the carpet. So when a rat moved into our neighborhood a couple of weeks ago, and he decided to take up residence over at neighbor Bill's house, it was up to Rusty to take action.

Here's how the big rat fight took place, and I had a perfect view from our kitchen window. Mr. Rat was drinkin' from neighbor Bill's birdbath...you know...the big marble one outside his kitchen window. Well, Mr. Rat was takin' his own sweet time,

drinkin', then playin' in the water, then washin' himself and dog-gone it, the only thing missing was him callin' for room service. Well, Rusty was stretched out on neighbor Bill's kitchen counter just mindin' his own business (the counter he's not supposed to sleep on, by the way, but he always does when neighbor Bill and Mrs. Bill are at work). Anyway, when Rusty saw that rat, you could see the fur on that cat's back stand up so straight he looked like a giant, orange fur ball. The next thing I knew, Rusty had disappeared from the window, ran from the kitchen into the garage, crawled out his little cat door, jumped over the fence and onto the roof, and then slowly crawled to the edge and looked straight down at the goings-on in that there bird bath. And let me tell you, the fireworks were about to begin, and I had a ring-side seat.

Rusty dove off that roof like a tennis ball droppin' out of the sky and landed right smack dab in the middle of that bird bath. Now, that bit about cats always landing on all fours is a big bag of hooey, because I've chased many a cat and saw them jump up and over our fence and land right on their little cat butts, and Rusty was no exception. He landed on his little orange rump, but he wasn't hurt none at all. And you know why? Because Mr. Rat cushioned the fall. Yep. He treated that rat like he was a trampoline. He bounced off that rodent and while

the rat was knocked to the ground right beneath that there bird bath, Rusty was free-fallin' into neighbor Bill's azalea bushes. Well, Mr. Rat hopped up and started staggerin' around like he had just stepped off a roller-coaster, and Rusty was shakin' his furry little cat head to sort of clear out the cobwebs. It was then they spotted one another, and Mr. Rat decided to skedaddle out of there like his tail was on fire. But just as the rat was scurrying through the bushes, Rusty made his move.

Rusty took a runnin' jump out of that there azalea bush like a cat with only one thing on his mind, and that was to have himself a rat burger for lunch. He dove after Mr. Rat, grabbed him by his tail, and held on for dear life. Which was exactly what Mr. Rat was tryin' to do on the other end of that there tail...he was tryin' to hold on to HIS dear life. Well, he started runnin' as fast as he could and his four little rat legs were spinnin' like they was wheels, except he was gettin' nowhere fast. And as Rusty was playin tug-of-war with Mr. Rat's tail, and tryin' to pull him in the opposite direction that Mr. Rat was plannin' on goin', the dad-blasted thing you ever did see happened.

Rusty went tumbling head over heels one way, and Mr. Rat took off like a bat chasin' bugs the other way, right down the street and into the sewer...which is where he belonged in the first place. And how did he get away from Rusty, since

that there cat had such a good grip on his tail? Rusty finally stopped turnin' summersaults and came to a rest sitting upside down against neighbor Bill's bird feeder. And you know what he had? He had Mr. Rat's tail still in his mouth! He pulled that sucker off, clean as a whistle. Now, I once heard the Mister tell a story about how he saw his dad, who was a dairy farmer, get so mad at a cow once because he wasn't goin' in the right direction, that he grabbed that cow's tail and pulled it so hard that it came right off in his hand, and he shook it in the air like a cowhide whip, which I suppose it was, now that I think about it. But I didn't think I would ever see a cat de-tail a rat. Until now, that is. And I was sittin' on the front row, and I witnessed the whole thing. And if I hadn't seen it with my own two dog eyes, I would have never believed it.

Imagine that…a de-tailed rat trying to swim down the sewer without his rudder, and a neighbor's cat with a hairy little souvenir. Who would have believed it?!

Quack?

Chloe and the Ducks

Hello...Belle here. When you humans think of a Labrador retriever, what comes to mind? A small, foo-foo little yapper like one of them Frenchie poodles with their hair all shaved and ribbons in their ears? Heck no. Or one of them hound dogs all covered with wrinkles and so many folds of skin you can get lost in? Nope. Or maybe one of them dogs who has one eyeball lookin' one way and the other eyeball lookin' the other way and a nose as flat as a dog tag? Goodness gracious no! Why, when the thought of a Lab pops into your head, you picture a beautiful animal diving into icy water retrieving a duck

just brought down by an early morning hunter. Or perhaps a dog playfully retrieving a tennis ball thrown into the backyard cement pond. Or maybe you think of a Lab swimming gracefully in the lake while the Mister is fishin' from the bank. In other words, when you think of me, you think of a great looking dog that not only loves water but understands that one of its main purposes in life is fetchin' just about anything, whether it's a ball or a stick or a dead duck. And since me and my sister fit all of these descriptions, the Mister and Missus just couldn't wait to take me and Chloe to the lake.

We were just pups at the time...about six months old...when the family drove us over to this big ol' pond. Not a real lake mind you, but a pond in the middle of a park on the other side of town. I fell in love with the place as soon as I hopped out of the backseat. There was grass and trees and picnic tables as far as I could see, and more smells than a dog could imagine. I was in puppy heaven! And what did I see swimmin' across that pond? Ducks! Hundreds of 'em. About this time my sister finally crawled out of the car and started runnin' in circles like she's prone to do, just a squattin' and a peein' to beat sixty. Why, she didn't weigh thirty pounds back then, and I bet twenty of 'em was pee. Anyway, after she watered just about every plant growin' in that park, she finally came over and joined me at the water's edge.

The Mister made sure both of us had our leashes and collars on real good, and he let me jump in first (after all, I'm the Alpha one around here, which means I get to do everything first). I dove in and immediately came up dog-paddlin'. I swam and swam as far as that leash would let me. I saw some ducks and tried and tried to reach those little feathered critters, but with that leash on, I just pretty much swam in circles. But that was the most fun I ever had in my life! As I crawled out of the water and shook about a gallon of the pond on the Missus, who didn't appreciate it near as much as the Mister did, my sister jumped in. Chloe loved the water, too, 'cause she started paddlin' all over the place, divin' under and swimmin' as far as that there leash would allow. I was really proud of my little sister, 'cause she appeared to be as good a swimmer as me. That is, until Donald and Daffy swam over to check out the situation. That's when I wanted to find the nearest trash barrel and hide.

Chloe spotted those two mallards swimmin' calmly over to her, and what does she do? Does she try to grab 'em, like any good Lab would do? Did she try to sneak up on 'em from below, grab their little tail feathers and drag them over to the Mister? Did she even act like a Lab? Heck no! My sister immediately turned into "St. Chloe", 'cause she almost walked on the water tryin' to get out of the pond and away from those big, scary ducks. She climbed up the bank, slippin' and slidin' all the way, until she was safe and sound back on the bank. But if that

wasn't bad enough, she then proceeded to twist her leash in and around the Mister and Missus' legs while tryin' to hide from them birds. Those ducks started quacking...I swear it sounded like they was laughin'...at my sister, mind you...and Chloe did everything she could to disappear, including trying to climb up the Mister's pants leg. He dropped her leash, grabbed her hind legs and proceeded to pull her head out of his pants. There was people sittin' at the nearby picnic tables...total strangers now... and they started laughin' and pointin'. One snotty little kid even walked over and asked the Mister what kind of dogs he had. When the Mister told him we was Labrador retrievers, he ran back over to his mom and dad, shakin' his head and giggling all the way. When he made it over to his table, I could see that he was tellin' his parents what the Mister had said...and they all burst out laughin'. Well, the Mister scooped us both up, told the Missus to come on, and we all marched over to the car without sayin' one word. He put us in the backseat, rolled up the tinted windows, put his sunglasses on, pulled his cap down over his eyes and drove like a greyhound out of there.

It's been seven years now, and we haven't gone back to that there pond even once...at least not during the daylight. It's one thing havin' a lab that's afraid of ducks. It's another thing having a dog that tries to climb inside your pants to hide. That's just totally embarrassin'.

Molly and Coconut

OK. Here's the dad-gum situation. Me and my sister Chloe aren't the only dogs in this here family any more. I don't mean the Mister and Missus done went and got another Lab or two...THAT we could handle. What I mean is that all of a sudden, like overnight or somethin', we done inherited two little yapper cousins. The Mister and Missus' son, Chris, done got himself married. That's not necessarily a bad thing in and of itself. I mean, the girl he married is a real little sweetie. She loves to scratch us behind our ears, and she's been known to rub our tummies 'til we're almost sound asleep. But there's some

serious baggage that came with that marriage, and their names are Molly and Coconut.

Coconut is what you call a Schnauzer, and Molly has a bunch of Rat Terrier in her....and I emphasize the word rat. Coco is actually an OK dog, if you can ignore her constant yapping and running around in circles. Chris says she's a little drama queen, but he usually says it where his wife can't hear him. Molly, on the other hand, is just a smooth runnin' little nut. All she wants to do is be a pest, clear and simple. When she and Coco come over to visit, she's immediately into my stuff. She eats my rawhide strips, she grabs our tasty pig ears and runs off with them and hides, she pulls every stuffed toy out of our box and carries them all over the house, and if you want to stretch out and take a quiet nap by the window with the sunlight coming in...well, forget about it.

Now, I simply don't put up with her shenanigans, but Chloe, for some reason, seems to actually enjoy her company. What's up with that? I mean, Molly will grab Chloe's tail and she doesn't mind it at all. She'll nip at her nose and it's fine and dandy. She'll run over, under and around the furniture at a mile a minute, and Chloe just goes right along with it. Why, Chloe even lets Molly eat out of her own food dish. Can you believe that? Sometimes I don't even think Chloe and I are related.

One time Molly tried to eat out of my bowl. She only did that once, though. I turned around and caught her right in the

Molly and Coconut

act, and you know what I did? I simply let out one of my barks, about six inches from her perky little button nose, and that little rat hound froze right in her tracks. She just fell right smack dab over and didn't move a muscle. I thought I killed her or somethin'. I mean, I looked down at her and she was stiff as a board. Then she slowly opened one eye, and I guess she realized that I wasn't going to eat her or somethin', and she was up and out of there like a scalded cat.

That was one of my best days ever.

Belle Has a Lump

Hi, folks…Belle here. Today the Mister had to take me to the doctor (he calls her a veterinarian…but if she pokes me with a needle one more time or sticks a cold thermometer where it completely disappears out of sight, if you know what

I mean and I'm pretty sure you do, well, I'm gonna call her an appetizer). Now, the reason I had to go visit her was because I've got some kind of lump or bump or something growing under my fur near my ribs…OK, I'm not really sure I have any ribs, 'cause I weigh over a hundred pounds and the Mister can't even find a hint of 'em when he tickles me…but he says I have no ribs because the Missus keeps giving us treats. Well, this doctor lady stuck two needles into this lump and I didn't enjoy it at all. Now mind you, I didn't whimper or growl or bark or nothin', cause us Labs are said to be stoic…whatever that means…but it hurt like nothin' you ever saw. Well, lately both the Mister and the Missus have been pretty worried about this lump, I don't know why 'cause they never tell me anything around here, but the word "cancer" keeps coming up. Why, the Missus even gets teary-eyed when she talks about it. But this morning, as I was saying, I went to the vet and she poked and prodded and stuck me with needles and everything else she could think of. Then she told the Mister that she'd call him with what she found out. Then she gave me a couple of dog biscuits, and I decided this vet lady is all right after all. As long as she keeps a supply of them biscuits on hand.

Well, to make a long story short, the vet lady just called, and that lump ain't nothin' to be worried about. It's called a cyst or somethin' or other. Basically, it's just a lump that nobody has to be bothered about. Which really made the Mister

happy…and the Missus, well, you should have seen her. She was almost as happy as the day she finally taught Chloe to sit, stay and go to the patio door when she needed to go outside. I learned these things right away, but like I've mentioned before, Chloe is one crazy dog…kinda slow like our two little yapper cousins, Molly and Coconut. We all know their porch light's on, but there sure ain't nobody home.

Well, that's my story for today...and if you learned anything at all, it's to make sure that if you own a dog...or heaven forbid... a cat lives with you, then it's your sworn duty to always take them to the vet for check-ups. The Mister takes me and my sister twice a year to be examined from head to tail, and you should take your furry friends, too.

But remember: it's the tail part of the exam where that thermometer thing can disappear. That's an amazing trick, if I do say so myself!

Molly and the Possum

Well folks, this is Belle...and I've now seen just about everything. I mean, I've seen my sister Chloe scared to death of ducks (just imagine...a Labrador retriever being afraid of DUCKS), and like I'm going to tell you later in this here book, I've seen a horse the size of a house pullin' a wagon load of people singin' Christmas songs one night and my crazy sister trying to climb up in that thing as it was travelin' along the neighborhood street (you should have seen them folks trying to bail out of that wagon...they all thought some kind of wolf or coyote was tryin' to join them for choir

practice). And I've seen Chloe scare the bejeebers out some door-to-door preacher fellas (more on that story a bit later, by the way). But I've never...and I repeat never...seen our little yapper cousin Molly try to single handedly wrestle with a possum. Until yesterday, that is.

Molly and Coconut, our two little yapper cousins that belong to the Mister and Missus' son Chris and his lovely wife Kamryn, came over yesterday to spend the weekend with us. Now them coming over to bunk with us is all well and good and no harm done...as long as Molly leaves my tennis balls and my rawhide bones alone...which she has learned to do...through much trial and error on her part...thank you very much. And, if I had to admit it, havin' them over for company can kind of be entertaining, in a strange sort of way. You see, Molly has a habit of runnin' lickety-split through the house chasing Coconut. I mean, that little rat terrier tears out after that Schnauzer and they chase each other a mile-a-minute throughout the house, over the furniture, under the beds, and around the corners like Junior in his NASCAR, all afternoon while me and Chloe just lie in front of the fire place watchin' the high-speed parade. And I must confess it IS quite amusing. But not near as funny as later in the day, when Mr. Possum showed up.

It seems we got us one of them rodents with a built-in pocket livin' in our backyard. Now, me and Chloe never seen the boy before, because...well...we spend most of our days and

nights inside the big brick air-conditioned dog house with the Mister and the Missus. And about the only time we go outside is when nature calls, if you know what I mean and I'm sure you do. And since our backyard ain't patrolled by me and Chloe much anymore, Mr. Possum just decided to move right in...or I should say 'right under'...our patio. And yesterday afternoon, Mr. Possum and Molly met one another, face-to-face.

Molly likes our backyard. She tends to "explore" a lot, which basically means she likes to stick her little button nose where it don't belong. We got trees and ivy and bushes and flowers and a bird bath and just all sorts of things a dog likes to get up close and personal with. And that was exactly what Molly was doin' when she discovered that tunnel leading under our patio. Now, rat terriers are scrappy little things, and Molly has what the Mister calls a "Napoleonic Complex", which is a mouthful of words that simply means she thinks she's bigger than she really is (and she WANTS to be, too)...which explains why she still has this death-wish of wanting to take one of my fried pig ears away from me, even WHEN I'M EATING IT, for Pete's sake (and one day I'm going to grant her that wish, if she's not careful). Anyway, yesterday afternoon Molly was snoopin' around the backyard when she found that there tunnel I was tellin' you about. And since rat terriers were trained a couple of hundred dog years ago to crawl into tight little

spaces to catch rats and rabbits and anything else livin' down in those holes...well, she just instinctively started to diggin'. And when I say diggin', I do mean diggin'. That little yapper started burying down in that tunnel until her little snub-nosed tail done disappeared. And the next thing I knew there were noises comin' from beneath that patio that sounded like sounds from a slaughter house. There were barks and growls and hisses and then dirt started flyin' out of that hole and out come Mr. Possum followed by Molly. And Molly had hold of that hairy little rodent's tail and wouldn't let go. I mean, that possum ran and spun around and shook that tail and Molly held on tight. She was bein' thrown side to side, all four feet off the ground, but she wasn't lettin' go for nothin'. That possum started runnin' through the bushes and in and out of the ivy and through the Missus' flower bed and then he tried to climb right up our big old oak tree and all the while Molly was hangin' on tight as could be. When that possum got about half way up the trunk of that tree, Molly dug her toenails into that tree bark and dadgum it if she didn't pull that possum out of that tree just before he reached that limb he was after. And both Molly and Mr. Possum fell to the ground with a 'thud' like you never heard before. Now, Molly and that possum just laid on the ground for a minute or two, and I thought they might be goners. But then Molly sat up, shook her little rat hound head and started examining that there rodent. She pushed him with her paws, nudged him with her nose, pulled on his raggedy old tail, and

nothin' happened. That hairy little fella was out like a light... not movin' a hair, nor breathin' a breath. Then Molly sat back down and I'm pretty sure she kind of started feelin' sad for that little rodent. I mean, she had only been doin' what she was raised to do...and that was to get rid of pests, and a possum is about as big a pest as there is. And while Molly was sittin' there feelin' sorry and all, you know what happened next? That possum opened one eye, jumped up, ran through the bushes and beneath the ivy and up and over our fence and down the alley. Molly didn't even see it comin', although I did, since I'm a seasoned hunter, and Molly is just a little yapper dog trained to get rid of rats and stuff.

You see, Mr. Possum was doin' what came naturally to him, and that's 'playing possum'. He knew that if he laid real still and sort of held his breath, that Miss Molly would just sniff him and then leave him alone...because she would think he was a goner. And that's exactly what he did...and that's exactly what she did. And while Mr. Possum was last seen waddling down the alley looking for his next meal, our little Molly was still sitting in the middle of the backyard tryin' to figure out what had just happened.

And I doubt if she'll ever learn. And why? Because she's a little yapper dog, and not a seasoned hunter like me.

A Den Just Isn't Big Enough for Two Labs and a Squirrel

The Walker household had a great Christmas. Santa found our house before our MasterCard and VISA bills arrived, so the way I figured it the holiday season was a success. Cathy had several surprises under the tree, and I got a nice new rod and reel to replace the one that somehow ended up at the bottom of Lake Dallas. Belle and Chloe had a fun Christmas too, receiving new tennis balls, a bag of fried pig ears (they love those disgusting

The Misadventures of Belle & Chloe

little things) and a sack of tasty peanut butter flavored rawhide strips. But I think what they enjoyed the most was Christmas Eve afternoon.

Cathy was out doing a little last minute shopping, I was home watching a college football bowl game, and the dogs were stretched out lazily by the fireside. Now, Chloe was on medication at the time for an itchy skin allergy (she's a Lab... what else is new?), and the pills tend to make her visit the back yard quite often, if you know what I mean and I think you do. And let it be known that when she has to go, she really has to go. I was on the den floor watching TV and both dogs were lying on their pillows and enthusiastically involved with one of their many chew toys. Well, Chloe had to go outside...again... so I got up and opened the back door for her...again. It was too cold to go outside and stand on the patio until she was finished, so I simply left the door open about a foot or so and went back to my football game. I knew that when Chloe was through she'd simply trot back inside and return to her pillow. Well, after a few minutes she came back inside the den and proceeded to play tug-of-war with Belle and one of her toys. I was too lazy to go over and close the door (plus, it felt nice to have the cool air filtering into the den), and so I just decided that I would simply wait until this goal line play was over and then I'd get up and close the door. The pups were gently nipping and tugging with one another, I was involved in

watching a quarterback option play, the door was open, a nice bit of cool air was drifting into the warm den, and all was right with the world.

And then World War III broke out.

A Texas gray squirrel the size of a small farm animal appeared on our patio, peered in through the door and, since he evidently enjoyed the Norman Rockwell scene, he just sat there examining things. I didn't immediately notice him, but Belle and Chloe caught his scent right away. Now, in order for you to appreciate the fiasco that was about to occur, you must first picture how our den was arranged. The patio door was about six feet to my left, next to the fireplace. The dogs were to my right about 7 feet away, the television was in the center of the room, and I was just an innocent bystander sitting right smack dab in the middle of what was about to become Armageddon. Both dogs let out a ferocious bark...they each weighed 85 pounds, so their barks probably weighed 10 pounds each...and they then made a flying leap over me and towards the open door in pursuit of Mr. Squirrel. Now remember, they only had about a dozen feet or so to clear from where they had been sitting to the outside door. But in between the dogs and the door were a coffee table, a footstool, a love seat, two lamps, a magazine rack, a pile of wood stacked against the fireplace, the television set, and me. And they managed to hit each and every object. It was

like something out of a cartoon (you know the one...where the coyote is trying to run so fast to catch the roadrunner that he's actually suspended in mid-air and his legs are moving so fast they're a blur). Well, the Lab parade zipped past me, knocked the foot stool about 2 feet in the air, moved the 300 pound love seat back about 4 feet, sent the firewood flying, knocked one of the lamps into the magazine rack and then both dogs bounded out the door with their tongues flapping in the breeze while the hairy little rodent easily and confidently ran up and over the fence, snickering all the way.

Belle and Chloe spent the rest of the afternoon barking, jumping and running all over the back yard trying to figure out what had just transpired, while I was busy trying to put the den back together before Cathy returned home.

I don't even know who won the football game.

Mouth-to-Snout Resuscitation

A few years ago, when me and Chloe were just pups, we did what pups did. We played games with one another just about all day long. We'd wrestle with one another, we'd chase each other, we'd bark at birds, we'd try to catch squirrels (never did come close to gettin' one of them rodents, neither). In other words, we played hard and fast from sun up to sun down...with plenty of naps in between, of course.

Now, one afternoon Chloe and I were wrestlin' on the patio, which was one of the things we loved to do most. And our favorite thing to do when wrestlin' was to grab the other by the collar and throw 'em down on the ground. Well, one day when we were especially rambunctious, my sister and I accidentally got twisted around one another and my collar just about choked me to death. No kidding! I thought for a minute or two I was a goner.

And if it wasn't for the Mister, I might not be tellin' this story right now. In fact, I'm gonna let the Mister tell you how it all happened, 'cause he can tell this story so good a magazine done published it. That's right! A magazine called *Just Labs* was gonna run a story about how to give what you call "mouth-to-mouth resuscitation" to a dog. Which is exactly what the Mister did to me that afternoon (although it was more like mouth-to-snout, since I was just a pup at the time and the Mister could pretty near put my whole muzzle in his mouth, which is kinda what he did). Anyway, this here magazine asked the Mister to write a story 'bout what happened to me, which he did, and they liked it so much they published it. And here it is:

Saving a Lab

New Year's Eve, 2000, started out like any other holiday weekend. My wife Cathy, was in Dallas shopping for a gift for her sister's upcoming wedding, our two nine month old chocolate Lab puppies were running and romping in our fenced backyard oblivious to the world going on around them, and I was comfortably in the den watching football on TV. All was right with the world. And then it happened.

All of a sudden I heard what sounded like a dog fight on our patio. I looked out the window and saw Chloe straddling over Belle, with her teeth wrapped around Belle's throat. Now, I almost had to look twice, because these two little Lab sisters love each other as much as they love us, and they would never intentionally harm one another. I ran out the back door, saw blood on the patio floor, and then I realized what had happened (and if I hadn't seen it for myself, I would have never believed it).

Like most puppies, Belle and Chloe love to rough house with one another, running non-stop, nipping, tumbling, chasing and wrestling with each other all over the back yard. But while playing this particular afternoon, Belle's collar somehow accidentally became caught in Chloe's mouth and the pups became entwined with one another. And the more they panicked, the tighter little Belle's collar became twisted around her neck, like a tourniquet. I jumped between these 60-pound pups and tried and tried to get Chloe's lower jaw free from Belle's collar. Finally, after what seemed like an eternity, Belle's collar opened and separated (fortunately, it was a snap-free collar...a belt-type latch would have been disastrous). Chloe,

frightened and confused as she could be, ran over to the other side of the patio, cowering behind her doghouse, and watched from a distance while I cradled her sister in my arms. Belle's collar had become so tight that she had lost consciousness. Her little eyes had rolled back up into her head, and her tongue was swollen and bleeding where she had bit it (her tongue somehow became caught between her teeth, and as her collar tightened, her jaws closed tighter and tighter). It was then that I realized that she was no longer breathing. I shook her and shook her, but to no avail. She lay in my arms like a rag doll. I then immediately began giving her mouth-to-mouth resuscitation. I remembered watching a piece on the Animal Planet TV channel months earlier, and I went to work on her, almost without thinking. I laid her on the patio, got her tongue clear and started breathing into her nose and mouth while massaging her chest. But nothing happened. She showed no response at all. No eye movement, no breathing, nothing at all.

Now, I'm a fairly religious guy, and I'm well aware what my Maker can do, and that's when God and I had a quick man-to-Man talk. I told Him that during my 51 years He knew that I had lost many a dog through car accidents, theft, disease, and old age. And that He knew what these two pups meant to my family and me. And that He also knew that I was not going to lose Belle to a freak accident like this. I asked Him

to give me strength and guidance, and to not let me give up... no matter what.

I then repositioned Belle and cradled her in my arms, placed her nuzzle against my face, and started breathing for her once again. I forced my air deep into her lungs, all the while massaging her chest, her legs, her sides. After what seemed like an eternity had passed, Belle choked a bit, opened her

eyes, crawled out of my arms and staggered to her feet. She shook herself...just like she does when we give her a bath... and staggered over to Chloe, who proceeded to nuzzle her face and lick her ears. They then both walked over to me and gave me the same greeting. The three of us sat on that patio and hugged each other for what seemed like the rest of the afternoon. Later that evening, both pups relaxed in our den, stretched out on their pillows in front of the fire with their tennis balls at their sides, as if nothing had ever happened. I, on the other hand, was still a nervous wreck wondering how the day might have turned out differently if I had not been home when our Labs needed me the most.

As every Lab owner knows, our dogs are always there when we need them at the end of a long work day, when we're tired or sad or lonely, or when we just need to see a cheerful face. Whatever the situation calls for, they're always there for us.

For once, I'm just glad I was able to return the favor.

Giving Your Dog CPR

Cardio-Pulmonary Resuscitation, or CPR, is a version of artificial respiration that includes assisting the heart to beat. The purpose of CPR is to keep oxygen moving to the lungs and blood circulating throughout the body. The directions contained here APPLY TO DOGS. While these instructions may be helpful in an emergency, it is best to always check with your veterinarian to establish the procedure that is best for your pet.

How To Administer CPR

- If your dog is not breathing, use your finger to clear any foreign object from the mouth.

- Tilt his head back to straighten the airway passage.

- Hold his mouth shut with one hand, and place your mouth over the dog's nose and mouth making sure the seal is tight.

- Blow into the nose while watching to see if his chest expands.

If his chest DOES NOT EXPAND, start over again by clearing your dog's mouth. If his chest DOES EXPAND, release your dog's mouth so it can exhale. Repeat the breathing procedure once every five seconds until your dog is breathing normally, or until your vet is available to begin treatment.

Heart Massage

IF YOU CANNOT DETECT A HEARTBEAT, YOU MUST PERFORM HEART MASSAGE IN CONJUNCTION WITH THE BREATHING

- **Put your dog on his right side.**
- **The heart is located in the lower half of the chest, behind the elbow of the front left leg. Place one hand below the heart to support the chest, place the other hand over the heart and compress gently.**
- **Depending on the size of your dog, apply pressure using both hands, with each compression lasting no longer than ½ second. The smaller the dog, the less force is needed. Do not damage the ribs.**
- **Repeat this procedure a total of 10 times. Then, if your dog is NOT breathing, perform CPR as described above.**
- **Alternate between the chest compressions (10 in a row) and one breath through your dog's nose.**
- **GET YOUR DOG TO A VETERINARIAN**

Saving your pet with CPR

With pets increasingly being treated like a member of the family, many owners are learning emergency techniques like CPR to keep their pet alive before bringing it to a veterinarian.

If there is no breathing and no pulse, begin CPR immediately.

Areas to check for pulse

Check for breathing and pulse
Check pulse using middle and index finger below the wrist, inner thigh (femoral artery), below the ankle or where left elbow touches the chest.

Look for other warning signs
- Gums and lips will appear gray-colored.
- Pupils will be dilated and not responsive to light.

Gums

Pupils

If not breathing, give breath to animal

Cats and small dogs
Place your mouth over its nose and mouth to blow air in.

Medium–large dogs
Place your mouth over its nose to blow air in.

Heimlich maneuver
If breath won't go in, airway may be blocked. Turn dog upside down, with its back against your chest. Wrap your arms around the dog and clasp your hands together just below its rib cage (since you're holding the dog upside down, it's above the rib cage, in the abdomen). Using both arms, give five sharp thrusts to the abdomen. Then check its mouth or airway for the object. If you see it, remove it and give two more rescue breaths.

Start compressions if no pulse
Lay animal on right side and place hand over ribs where its elbow touches the chest. Begin compressions. Do not give compressions if dog has pulse.

Animal size	Compress chest	Compressions per breath of air
Cat/small dog (Under 30 lbs.)	1/2-1 inch	5
Medium–large dog (30–90 lbs.)	1–3 inches	5
Giant dog (over 90 lbs.)	1–3 inches	10

Repeat procedure
- Check pulse after 1 minute and then every few minutes.
- Continue giving CPR until the animal has a pulse and is breathing.
- Stop CPR after 20 minutes.

SOURCE: American Red Cross

Chloe and the Door-to-Door Preachers

Hi there. This is Chloe, and it's finally my turn to tell another one of these stories my way...not the way my sister Belle explains things...but the way I do. If you listened to the way she rattles on and on regarding some of the things we do, you'd think she was the smartest dog in the neighborhood and I was the dumbest. I mean, everyone knows the smartest dog in the

neighborhood is this German Shepherd that lives about two streets over, but that's another story.

I don't know what the summers are like where you're from, but here in Texas it's best to stay out of the sun, especially if you wear a fur coat year-round like me and my sister do. And the best place we've found to hang out during the heat of the day is in the front hallway of the Mister's big dog house, right by this glass door that lets just enough sunlight through to help a Lab sleep all day long. And the hall floor is made out of something called I-talian tile. I'm not sure what that is, but it sure is cool during the summer, and to stretch out on that nice cool floor with the sunlight coming through is almost as good as watching this Blue Jay that lives in our oak tree chase our neighbor Bill's cat, Rusty. I swear, I could watch that bird dive bomb that cat all day long. Why, I bet Rusty has been pecked and scratched and chased up trees and over fences so many times that he's probably used up 6 or 7 of his 9 lives by now. And dog-gone-it if I haven't done forgotten what I was talkin' about now (Belle tells me my mind wanders so much that I can't walk and chew rawhide at the same time).

Oh...I was talking about sleeping in the hallway. Well, the other day Belle and I were stretched out, snoring away, when these here two guys come up to the porch. I later heard the Mister tell the Missus that we must have been visited by some door-to-door preachers, whatever that means. The Missus

The Misadventures of Belle & Chloe

asked him how he figured that out, and he said something about some little pamphlets were scattered all over the front lawn and down the sidewalk. Now neither one of 'em could figure out how those little books got there, but I sure knew, and I wasn't tellin'. Until now, 'cause this is my story and I can do whatever I want. So here's the deal...

I'm layin' in the hall, minding my own business, half asleep and half awake (according to Belle, I tend to stay that way most of the time, and to be honest with you, she may be right about this one). Anyway, Belle is sound asleep, and I'm just kind of relaxin' there, like I say, just minding my own business, when these two preacher fellas park their bikes by our big oak tree and come walking up to the porch and ring this dad-blasted bell that for some reason tends to make a racket every time somebody comes to the front door. Well, Belle could pretty much care less if someone rings the bell, knocks on the door, climbs through a window or whatever...as long as they don't interrupt her snoring. I mean, if there's a dog that ever needed her beauty sleep it's that one. But hey now...this is the Mister and Missus' dog house, and nobody but nobody is allowed inside without their say so except me and my sister. And that for dog-gone sure means these two Yahoos. So, what do I do? I "spring into action", and when I say "spring", I do mean "spring". As soon as that doorbell rang, I bounced up off that Italian tile and let out one of my barks, which I've been told can

The Misadventures of Belle & Chloe

cause the fur to fall off a cat's tail at 20 yards, which I'm proud to say I've done on more than one occasion. Well, I started barkin' and leapin' and I hit that glass door with my front paws and those poor preacher boys had a look on their face that reminded me of the expression I saw on our neighbor Bill's cat that winter morning the Mister started up his car and that sucker was sleeping under the hood. He came flyin' out from under there like his tail was on fire...and now that I think about it, I'm pretty sure it was on fire. Anyway, I laughed so hard Gravy Train came out my nose, but that's another story. Those little booklets went flyin' about ten feet in the air, one of the guys tripped and fell behind the Missus' crepe myrtle while the other one staggered backwards toward the curb waving his arms and clutching his chest and mumbling something about "I'm comin' home, Lord". The last I saw of those two preacher boys was them runnin' down the street, pretty much tripping over one another.

They still haven't come back to pick up their bicycles.

How to Beg...A Lab's Point of View

Most folks think us Labs are experts in swimmin' and divin' and retrievin' things...which we are...but let me tell you this about that: there's ONE thing that we are lord and masters of, and that's how to beg! And if there's a dog in this here household who's truly gifted in this area, it's my sister, Chloe.

Chloe is so good at beggin', that she's got it down to a fine art. Why, she's even known throughout the neighborhood as havin' her begging categorized. In other words, she has a different beg depending on the situation. And that's truly remarkable, if you ask me. I mean, this has

obviously taken years of refinement, and she now has it down to perfection.

Allow me to explain just what I mean.

Chloe's first type of beg is what she calls the "Please Feel Sorry for Me" beg. This type of beg starts out with the "guilt look", maintained by constant eye contact, and followed up with the "pitiful look". When Chloe applies this beg to the Missus, she not only will give my sister the last morsel off her plate, but she'll give her a great ear scratch, too. This is the easiest type of beg to perform, which is why she saves it for the Missus. This beg never works on the Mister, believe me.

A second type of beg is called the "Drooling" beg. When Chloe applies this beg, there's no direct eye contact involved. Instead, she licks her lips and drools just a bit, which causes her to look starved. And in order to seal the deal, she'll apply the double drool, which is most impressive. The double drool will cause even the most stubborn person (i.e. the Mister) to offer up a tidbit.

Her third type of beg is the "Lay Down on the Floor and Look Sad" beg. When using this one, Chloe again won't use any type of direct eye contact. Instead, she'll lie flat on the floor...maybe with her chin on her front paws for extra effect...and she will then inch very slowly toward the

Mister or Missus. Neighborhood dogs have been known to bark and wag their tails non-stop in appreciation when they've seen her in action using this one.

She calls this fourth type of beg, her "Pin Your Ears Back" beg. This one requires complete concentration because it involves pleading eyes, along with a head tilt and a whine while offering up one of her "I love you, man" expressions while pinning her ears back. This is a difficult one to master, simply because so much is involved in such a short time. Try it yourself and you'll see what I mean.

The following beg is one I really like. Why? Because it involves me, of course. This is called the "Tag Team" beg or the "Buddy" beg, and it requires both of us. For this beg, each of us has to apply the pleading look, with raised eyebrows, and we "grin" by drawing back our lips. A little drool helps, too, along with wiggling our butts. (A wiggling butt and a grin offer a killer effect, by the way... but you don't want to use it too often or else the Mister or Missus will catch on when they're being blind-sided by two Labs.)

The "Don't You Want to Play With Me?" beg is great to use after the Mister or Missus has been gone all day and they already sort of feel guilty about leaving us home all alone (although we don't mind having the run of the house one bit). For this one, Chloe must have a prop to use...

she has to find something to hold in her mouth, such as a tennis ball (and more than one is most helpful) or a Frisbee (or...again...Frisbees). Now, in order for this beg to work, Chloe has to use good behavior, such as sitting while begging. And guilt...use lots of guilt. If the Mister or Missus looks as though they're about to fall for it...but maybe not completely...just before they turn and walk away, she "sets the hook"...and to do this, while sitting politely with a mouthful of tennis balls, she starts stamping her front feet and wagging her tail and wigglin' her Lab butt. Once all the above is accomplished, the deal is sealed.

And last...but not least...is what she calls her "Combo Beg". The "Combo" is a combination of several of the above begs. This is the "big gun". The one she pulls out of her bag of begs when nothing else seems to work (Chloe usually saves this one to use on the Mister for that early Saturday morning when he wants to do nuthin' but sleep). For this one, Chloe will pin her ears back, get a bit of drool going while offering a grin, and then, while lying flat on the floor with her chin on her front paws, looks directly up at him with those big, brown sad eyes of hers. And then for the finishing touch, she'll walk directly over to his side of the bed, sits and places her left paw (my sister is left-pawed, by the way) up on the bed just a few inches from the Mister's nose. This big gun works every time.

Well, there you go. You now know the fine art of begging. Treat this information carefully because you don't want to over do it. You never know when you'll need to pull that "big gun" out of your own bag of begs.

"Don't You Want to Play With Me?" Beg

"The Combo" Beg

There's a Squirrel in the Flowerbed (and powdered dog pee, too)

Part 1

It's 5 a.m. on a Sunday morning, Belle and Chloe are sound asleep, and I'm writing this story to share with you. And why am I up at 5 a.m. on a Sunday morning you may ask? Because I'm on squirrel watch.

For the last two weeks, I've been working on a new flowerbed in our backyard. It's just a little thing, about 12 feet by 5 or 6 feet, curves a bit here and there, and takes up a portion of the backyard where I haven't been able to grow any grass. I tilled the area, worked some peat moss in, then a bit of organic fertilizer, and got it all prepared for a spring flower bed. You see, I found out several months ago that Cathy's granny had an iris flower garden years ago, and Cathy loves irises because of that reason, so I've planted irises, daffodils, tulips and crocuses in this little flower bed...she'll see it all next March when the little suckers start blooming... hopefully.

And the word "hopefully" is exactly why I'm up at 5 a.m. on squirrel watch.

Yesterday afternoon while I was about to grill a plate of hot dogs in my backyard, I decided to water my flowerbed. It was then that, to my horror, I noticed a handful of neatly dug holes...empty holes...where the bulbs were removed with surgical precision. I immediately walked around the corner of the house to turn off the water, when I spied a half-eaten bulb at the foot of one of my oak trees. I looked up into the tree, and two beady little eyes...little red devil eyes...were staring right back at me. Mr. Squirrel was just casually sitting on a limb happily munching on what was left of one of my tulip bulbs... an $8 tulip bulb mind you...just chattering away. And if this humiliation wasn't bad enough, the little rodent then tossed the remains right back down at me while cackling the entire time. Not a cute little cackle, like Chip and Dale used to do in the cartoons, but a chatter that sends a chill down your spine. In fact, a maniacal laugh best describes his vicious little sound.

Feeling helpless, I immediately went to the Internet to find out what keeps squirrels out of one's garden. After searching and searching, I finally came up with the solution: dried dog urine. It seems that there's a company out there that sells dried animal urine guaranteed to keep just about any type of animal out of your garden. If armadillos are eating your plants, spread dried coyote urine around the area and the critter will stay away. If raccoons are a problem, dried fox urine will do the trick. And if small rodents are being a pest (such as rabbits, mice and SQUIRRELS), then dried dog urine is guaranteed to keep the little demons out of your hair. For $15 a can, mind you.

But what bothers me almost as much as paying $15 for a can of dried dog pee, is that I've got two 100 pound chocolate Labs RIGHT THERE IN THE BACKYARD, thank you very much. And Chloe alone has about 15 gallons of pee in her at any particular time, which is like over a hundred bucks on the "keep the critters away" market. So why won't she pee in my flower bed? When she was a puppy, she peed just about everywhere else around here...in the den, the kitchen, under the coffee table, in our clothes hamper, on one of Cathy's shoes in her closet (she almost wouldn't have had anything left to pee with again if Cathy had caught her before I did). But will she help me keep the squirrels out of my flowerbed? NO. Will she even bark if she sees a squirrel? Not if the little sucker is having a picnic in the middle of the night, because that must be during

her off-hours, since she sleeps harder than a rock during the night. And during the morning. And during the afternoon.

And by the way...where is Belle during all this? Does she sleep on the patio, which is about 5 feet from the flowerbed? No. Does she sleep in the insulated, hand-made air-conditioned dog house that I built for them? (Yes...I did say air-conditioned and no, she doesn't sleep there.) Her current bed of choice is under one of our 8 foot Elephant Ear plants, where the mulch is nice and soft and cool...where she can turn her back to the yard and where she can completely ignore her strange little sister Chloe.

That's why I'm up at 5 a.m. on a Sunday morning, trying to catch the squirrels from robbing me blind of big bucks of bulbs.

Part 2

Well, as I mentioned in the previous story, the day after I planted all those bulbs in my new flowerbed, Mr. Squirrel made a midnight visit and had a nice little moonlight picnic. I decided to ignore it for one night, but then the next morning the little rodent struck again, so I get on the Internet to find out what product keeps squirrels away, and that's when I discovered the answer to my problems: Dried Dog Pee.

But after the SECOND night of feasting, I decided I couldn't wait for the pee to arrive so I went to the hardware store

and bought a roll of plastic netting. I came home, spread the netting across my flowerbed and staked it down nice and secure. The next morning...all was OK. I could see little squirrel foot prints around the side of bed, but he couldn't dig through the netting. The following day I found the same thing...no holes dug, just little foot prints (the pee arrived that afternoon, but I decided I didn't need to use it, so I stored it in my garage for the spring, when the bulbs start to come up and I'll then have to remove the netting). Then this morning I went out and lo and behold, there were 3 pecans left on the netting in a nice, neat little circle. Now, I don't know if the little critter had a picnic during the night and he was using the plastic netting as a table, or this was his way of apologizing to me for all the trouble he had caused. I imagine it was the former, but I'll assume it was the latter.

But this afternoon when I got home from work, I went outside to feed Belle and Chloe, and Belle had lifted and removed one corner of the netting and was stretched out in the cool, damp mulch. She thought she was in heaven, just sprawled out in the moist dirt. I hollered at her to get up and out of my flowerbed immediately, and after about 10 minutes of stretching and yawning and rolling one last time in the mulch, she then walked over to the patio and stretched out. I replaced the netting and staked everything back in place. I then went into the garage...and got a can of powdered pee.

I decided that if I sprinkled the pee all over the flowerbed, the squirrel would quit having picnics and Belle and Chloe would certainly leave the flowerbed alone. I shook that can of pee powder all over that flowerbed, and then stepped back to admire my one-upmanship. I was so proud of myself: I had designed a nice little flowerbed, tilled it up, planted all sorts of beautiful spring bulbs, placed a net across it in a very neat manner, and then spread my can of dog pee all throughout.

And as I looked upon several man-hours of work, Chloe casually walked across the flowerbed, sat down in the middle of it, scratched behind her ear, yawned, bent down, sniffed the powdered urine, and proceeded to squat and pee all over my flowerbed. Then she did a second bodily function that seemed like it took 5 minutes to perform. Afterwards, she walked back to the patio, stretched out under the ceiling fan, curled up and went to sleep.

The squirrel now looks like a very small problem compared to the gift that Chloe left on top of my flowerbed.

Top 10 Ways I Know I'm Owned by a Chocolate Lab

10 I've convinced myself that everything I own looks good in brown...couch, chair, bedspread, recliner, carpet, double oven, fireplace mantle, car seats, and all my clothes.

9 I find a puddle of water on the kitchen floor, and I'm thrilled to discover that it's just a leak in the washing machine hose.

8 I've convinced myself that I actually enjoy having two 100 pound Labs crawl in bed with me, and I've persuaded my wife that "there's room to spare". Yeah, right.

7) I decide to take a nap on the couch rather than on my comfy recliner, because Belle has already claimed the chair and she doesn't want to move.

6) I really don't mind walking out to the mail box on a frigid day without a jacket, because Chloe is sleeping in front of the coat closet and "she just won't get out of the way".

5) I just KNOW that there's a Lab on the other side of my morning newspaper, staring me down, pleading to go for a walk...and I decide I've read enough...even though I haven't even made it to the sports section yet...but that some "fresh air" would do me some good.

4) I have resigned myself that all the food on my plate is never all mine.

3) I've convinced myself that throwing a tennis ball across the backyard to absolutely no one with less than four legs for over an hour is actually good exercise for my arm.

2) I've convinced myself that picking up a grocery bag of dog poop in the backyard every freakin' day is good for my lower back muscles.

The Misadventures of Belle & Chloe

And the #1 way I know that I'm owned by a chocolate Lab…

1) At Christmas time, I completely rearrange the den so that the Christmas tree won't be in the dogs' way when they go in and out the back door, and I don't mind picking up decorations sprayed around the room like machine-gun fire due to a wickedly wagging tail.

Belle and Chloe's Memorial Day Picnic

I got up bright and early Memorial Day morning to put a brisket on my BBQ smoker out in the backyard. The hunk of meat was so big that I cut it in half, figuring I'd cook both halves and freeze one for a rainy day. Now, it takes about a half day to cook a 10 pound brisket, and by around the 5th hour of smoking and basting, little Chloe had salivated almost a river. She would follow me from the patio door to the smoker like a parade every time I would go out to check the meat...hoping she would somehow get a morsel. Belle on the other hand, who mainly likes to sleep in the shade or bark at the squirrels... not getting up and chasing them mind you, but just kind of

rolling over, raising her head and letting out a bark or two, so that the little rodents knew they could visit, but they couldn't move in…well, Belle was just pretty much annoyed at her sister's constant slobbering.

Anyway, when the briskets were done, I placed both of them on the grill's built-in shelf to "rest", so the juices could settle deep inside the meat before carving. Now, I've done this a million times…putting the steaks or briskets or hot dogs or whatever I'm grilling on the shelf that's built into the front of the grill… and nothing has ever happened to the food (the shelf is an extension of the grill…about 3 feet off the ground). Belle and Chloe know they can look, but they never, ever touch. And it's at this point in the story that I should tell you that Chloe's been on a diet for the last few months, and I suppose the temptation was just too much. So here was her plan:

She brought me their tennis ball and dropped it at my feet. Now, this means that she and Belle are telling me to toss the ball up on the roof of our house so that it'll roll down and they can catch it. So I threw the ball up on the roof, and both of the dogs started playing "catch and retrieve".

The dog that caught it would bring it back to me so that I would throw it again on the roof. Which I did. Time after time after time. About the ninth or tenth time I did this, I noticed that Belle was the only one catching the ball. I looked around for Chloe and found her under the shrubs attacking one of my briskets!

The sneaky thing had "lured" me into playing catch with her sister, while she snuck around behind me and took one of my briskets off the shelf. And as soon as Belle noticed what had happened, she immediately left me holding the ball, quite literally, and joined her sister under the shrubs for their own personal Memorial Day picnic dinner. It was so funny, I couldn't be mad...after all, it pretty much appeared that Chloe had master-minded the entire thing, from bringing me the ball in the first place, to acting like she wanted to play catch, to sneaking around behind me and stealing a hunk of beef.

I'm just surprised she didn't ask for the potato salad.

Looking at Christmas Lights

My sister Chloe and I did somethin' last night that was just about as much fun as two dogs could have, not counting that afternoon when we was watchin' out the kitchen window at our neighbor Bill's cat, Rusty, as he pounced on a squirrel that was busy nibbling on a corn cob feeder. Ol' Rusty missed that little hairy rodent by a good foot and wound up diving right smack-dab into the big marble bird bath beside neighbor Bill's azalea bushes. That cat came out of that there bird bath like one of them rockets fired out of one of them underwater Navy boats. Why, Chloe and I laughed so hard we had the hic-cups for durn near a half hour.

Anyway, what we did last night was what the Mister and Missus call "lookin' at Christmas lights". We all piled into the Mister's car and rode over to where the Mister calls "the rich part of town", and brother let me tell you somethin': he ain't wrong about that, because I never seen so many big brick dog houses in my dog life, and every one of 'em was covered with about a zillion lights (now me being a dog and all, I can't really count too good, so I'm just estimatin' on that zillion lights figure). Anyway, these houses had houses on top of each other! They were what you call two story and three story houses. Houses that almost reached the sky! And dog-gone it if there wasn't a fire hydrant in front of just about every other one of these big fancy homes. That's like a Labrador's dream come true. We tend to fancy them hydrants, and I don't think I need to tell you why 'cause I'm pretty sure you've seen us in action before. My sister Chloe has enough pee in her at just about any given time that she can water just about every flower, every hydrant, every tree and every blade of grass within a couple of city blocks. I mean, you put her in a new place with new smells and all she does is run, squat and pee...run, squat and pee. It's enough to make you dizzy just watchin' her in action.

Now, to get back to seein' them lights last night. We all drove around until the Missus found just the right neighborhood for us to have a look-see. Me and Chloe...and especially the Mister...couldn't really understand exactly what she was

looking for, since all those houses pretty much looked the same to us, but she's the Missus, and when the Mister says it's "all about her", well, he's pretty much tellin' it like it is. Ain't nobody in that car happy until the Missus is...which is actually the way the Mister wants it, although he'll never admit it. But when we finally found just the right neighborhood, I gotta admit it was well worth the trip.

Each big ol' house was lit up like it was in the middle of the day, and besides those zillion lights I was tellin' you about, each yard was lit up too. Can you imagine that? Lights running up the walls, over and up and down the roof, in the bushes and trees, and in the yards! Why, Chloe and I ain't never seen anything like it in all our dog-years. At one house there was a lighted up cow and a sheep and a donkey and what the Mister called camels (which just looked like fancy cows to me). And at another house there were deer that were lit up and movin' their heads all about, and one even had a red nose. Scared the bejeebers out of Chloe, by the way. She ain't never seen a deer with headlights before, and I've gotta admit that sucker gave me a start, too. But nothin' got our attention more than what was about to come down the street right in front of where that camel was parked (and if the Mister had seen it before Chloe and I did, I think he would have hauled us back to the car as fast as he could).

Chloe saw it first, and for those of you who have met her, you know Chloe doesn't run...she bounces from here to there, all the time wavin' that 5 pound tongue of hers in the breeze with slobber sprayin' everyone within sight. Anyway, she leaped so high and so quickly that her leash came out of the Missus' hands, and once that happened, I decided it was my turn to make a break for it, too. Which didn't happen of course, 'cause the Mister had hold of my leash, and he had me sit so quick my tail popped me in the back of my noggin and I durn near got tail-lash. But my little sister was free as the breeze and was just a tearin' out down the sidewalk to check out this dad-gum animal that was the size of one of them parade floats we saw on TV the other morning. I mean, this four-legged critter was just a clip-cloppin' down the street pullin' a wagon that was all lit up just like them houses. And dog-gone it if there weren't folks in that wagon just a singin' Christmas songs and laughin' and just as happy as they could be...that is, until my sister tried to climb in that wagon with 'em. That was about the time they tended to lose that there Christmas spirit.

Now let me explain the picture here for you folks who might still be thinking about that deer with headlights a few houses back. We've got this here Clydesdale pullin' a lit-up wagon full of folks and just proudly marchin' down the street. And then we've got a hundred pound chocolate Lab trying to climb up into that wagon simply wantin' to see what was going on. And

we've got a wagon load of people screamin' and hollerin' that there's a coyote or wolf or skunk or somethin' trying to have 'em for Christmas dinner. Now, I can see it being a coyote or a wolf...them being my cousins and all...but mistakin' my little sister for a skunk...well, that's just an insult, if you ask me.

Anyway, about that time the Mister arrived on the scene, with me in tow, and he single-handedly lifted Chloe by her rear end and out of that wagon while apologizing to just about everybody...the folks in the back of that wagon, the driver, and even that there Clydesdale (who actually was kinda enjoyin' everything that was going on). Well, the folks riding in that there carriage done quit singin' and was sayin' words I had only heard the Mister say when me or my sister would accidently forget to ask to go outside when we had to go but figured it was just too durn cold. But the Mister didn't hang around to visit. He grabbed me and Chloe and high-tailed it back to the car where the Missus was already sittin' with her coat up over her eyes and just prayin' that if we ever got home she'd never ask to go look at Christmas lights again.

Well, that was just about the most fun Chloe and I have ever had at Christmastime. Now we can't wait for New Year's.

There's a New, Pink Addition to the Family

Now here's the deal: this big old brick dog house is just the perfect size for the Mister, the Missus, and me and my sister Chloe. And, if I have to admit it, there's still enough room for an occasional visit from our two little doofus cousins, Molly and Coconut. But that's it! Enough is enough! And why am I sayin' this? Because a brand new visitor has arrived on the scene.

It seems as though the Mister and Missus' son, Chris...and his sweetie pie wife Kamryn...done went and got themselves a little pink human. That's right. Kamryn done had herself a baby! Not a baby Labrador, or a baby Schnauzer, or even a baby Rat Terrier (can you imagine that...another little Molly

runnin' crazy through this house?). Why, me and Chloe could probably handle that. But this little pink, wrinkly, cryin' thing is just too strange. And the different smells that little sucker puts out of that little body is just unbelievable...and you know how us dogs love different smells...but some of these odors can make a train take a dirt road, if you know what I mean.

But that's not all. When Pinky comes to visit, this little thing just has to have everybody's attention throughout the house. I mean, used to be, if I was hungry or needed to go outside or wanted to play ball with someone, well, either the Mister or the Missus or Chris just couldn't wait to take care of my every need. And if Chloe needed to go outside...and when she needs to go outside, believe me, she needs to GO outside...why, the Mister couldn't get to the patio door fast enough. But once that little pink thing arrived on the scene, me and Chloe were pretty much forgotten about. At least that's the way it seemed at first. I mean, all he did was just lay there...hardly movin' at all...just kind of squirming and screeching and laughing and stuff. But that's about it. I mean, at first, Pinky couldn't even move off that blanket of his. He'd just lay there and drool and giggle and make those smells I was tellin' you about. But that was then.

Now that little Pinky is old enough to crawl around on all fours... kind of like me and Chloe actually...then he sort of enters our world, and evidently he sort of sees things from our point of

view, because all he does is crawl over to us and screeches and giggles and laughs so much at us that sometimes milk comes out his nose (which is a pretty good trick, if you ask me). I mean, we don't even have to do anything...just sit there and look at Pinky, and he starts cacklin' like a chicken. And no matter where we go in the house, he comes crawlin' right after us, just laughin' all the way. And when the three of us get tired of playin' with one another, we all lie down in the corner and take a nap together, which evidently everyone in this house thinks is just as cute as can be because they're constantly taking pictures of the three of us.

Anyway, now that Pinky no longer sits there on the carpet all propped up on a pillow like he's one of my stuffed toys, he's sort of proven that he's OK to have around. In fact, the first time Pinky tried eating oatmeal and threw it on the floor, the Missus thought he was just bein' cranky...but me and my sister knew otherwise. This was Pinky's way of sharin' his food. And the way to a Labrador's heart is definitely through her stomach. And once Pinky started sharin' all his food with me and Chloe, well, we welcomed him into the family with open paws.

Yep, things are going to be fine and dandy around here.

The Mister and the Bassinette

Hi folks...Belle, here. It seems with the new edition to the family...that little pink thing that Chris and Kamryn done brought home named 'Jake'...well, it seems like Jake has caused a lot of commotion between the Mister and the Missus (and you already know that the Missus is going to win out on just about

The Misadventures of Belle & Chloe

every discussion that goes on in this here big brick dog house of ours).

Anyway, it seems that now the Missus has determined that the Mister needs to go buy just about everything known to humans regardin' the keeping of a little pink crawly thing. And this includes a little bed and somethin' called a playpen and a changin' table (I can't wait to see what that there table changes into...maybe a hamburger?) and even these soft, cloth things that you tape...TAPE, I say...to Jake's little behind, which I suppose means he doesn't have to go outside after he eats, if you know what I'm referrin' too. Heck...this kid doesn't have to do nothin' to get fed around here...just squeak a little and his mom goes and turns on her faucets and Jake turns into one happy kid. Amazing! Why, I remember when my sister Chloe and I were about as tiny as Jake and still hanging out with all our other brothers and sisters...did we have a bed like Jake's? Heck NO...we slept in a box with a towel. And did we have a playpen? Heavens NO...we had the entire back yard to play in. And did we have this here changin' table? WHAT on earth for? We never changed into nothin'. Probably because there's nothin' better to change into than bein' a Lab, anyway. And these diaper things? I don't even want to GO there, thank you very much (I mean, where would we put our tail?).

So the Mister goes out shoppin' and comes back with, what the Mister calls, an "All-in-One Nursery". And was the Mister ever proud of himself! He told the Missus that this thing starts out as a playpen, then turns into somethin' called a 'bassinette', and then it even turns into that there changin' table I was tellin' you about. Well, this I gotta see...which is pretty much the exact same words the Missus said.

The next thing I know, the Mister has all these furniture pieces back in the bedroom spread out all over the bed, all lined up neat and orderly...and the Mister wants it to stay that way. And how do I know this? Because Chloe done come in here to see what was goin' on...probably thinkin' that food might be involved... and she done hopped up on the bed while the Mister was layin' all these parts out. And when that 100 pound dog landed in the center of the bed, tongue just a wavin' in the breeze throwin' slobber from here to there and grinnin' like she done solved some world problem or somethin'...well, every piece and part to that there bed or playpen or changing table or whatever the heck it is went everywhere...and I do mean EVERYWHERE. The Mister then tried to grab Chloe, and she thought he was wantin' to play, and she started dartin' around, over and under that there bed and what pieces of furniture were still on it now started ricocheting around the bedroom, hittin' the dresser, the mirror and when one piece hit the Mister's big TV, he just threw

up his hands and asked the Missus to "come take care of HER dog"...and both us dogs know the Mister's in a bad mood when we become HER dogs...so we skedaddled out of that there bedroom and back into the kitchen where the Missus was getting ready for tomorrow's Thanksgiving dinner...and that there kitchen is where we'd rather be anyway, especially this time of the year.

So the Mister now starts gathering up the pieces of furniture and starts puttin' the thing together, and because of some of the words comin' out of the bedroom, I figured things weren't goin' too well (in fact, the Missus told both of us to stay out of that room, if we knew what was good for us, and brother did we ever).

Well, about an hour or so later, the Missus goes to check on the Mister and to see how the playpen thing looks. And it looks like it's a playpen still all spread out on the bed. I mean, there are parts that don't even go to the thing scattered around the room. The place looks like some science project done exploded or somethin'. And then the Mister says that the next time he's about to buy somethin' that says "No Tools Required", and states that "Anyone can put it together"...well, just take him by the hand and lead him back to the car.

But now...about 3 hours later...along with the Mister's three broken fingernails, a cut big toe (not sure how that happened), and one finger with the skin all gone (thanks to the instructions stating "For 7B, insert the wheel 'lightly but firmly' into said leg while pushing down on the release pin, while carefully noting the direction of said pin into said leg"), the contraption was FINISHED. And the Mister, grinnin' wide from ear to ear done rolled that thing into the den to show it off to the Missus. And was he ever proud of himself...that is, until the Missus said the playpen's mattress had to be removed and inserted into the bassinette part, because Jake was too tiny to use the playpen but that he would enjoy layin' in that there bassinette. And so the Mister would now have to remove the changin' table, which was connected to the side of the bassinette, which was connected to the side of the playpen, which had to have one of its sides removed to take out the mattress. Which means all of a sudden, there would be a zillion pieces of furniture spread out all over the room again.

And just what is the Mister goin' to do now? The last thing I heard was him laughin' like a crazy person, and sayin' somethin' about handing it all off to Chris tomorrow, because he's the kid's father, and that it's his chosen duty to put things like this together for his baby son, because "I've done served my time" raisin' Chris in the first place, and that "I've been there

and done that", and that Chris should now have the pure fun and enjoyment of putting Jake's stuff together...from now "until the kid goes off to college!"

Well, that's a good idea if you ask me, but I sure didn't see no 'enjoyment' on the Mister's face about 4 hours ago when Chloe hit that there bed runnin' and gunnin'. Nope...didn't see any enjoyment at all (except Chloe seemed to be having a pretty good time).

And now tomorrow, Chris gets to have some of this fun. I can't wait.

I love this kid!

Jake is 2 years old...and Belle is 10

We're Going to the Parade...I think!

Me and my sister Belle got all excited last week, and I gotta say, it was pretty much my fault. I mean, it was an honest mistake, but still...it was a pretty big error on my part. I thought I heard the Mister say we were all going to the PARADE,

and I thought, 'how great is that? Me and my sister are goin' DOWNTOWN to watch the parade.' Why, it's been a month of Sundays since we got to go watch one of them city parades. But I remember it like it was yesterday. There was bands and pretty girls and clowns that scared the bejeebers out me the first time I saw 'em, plus there was these trailer things they call floats. Why, there was even big horses like me and Belle saw last Christmas when I tried to climb up in that there carriage pulled by a Clydesdale and all those people in the back of that wagon had been singin' Christmas songs and all...until they saw me half way up in one of them lady's laps. I mean, all I wanted was some of that popcorn she was eatin'. My, that old lady sure could scream. I think she hit notes only us dogs could hear.

But lo and behold, it wasn't a parade we were going to get to go to. It was somethin' called gettin' SPAYED. And let me tell you somethin' about that there spaying process. Although it's sure not as much fun as chasin' squirrels or possums or rabbits, if you've got a dog or a cat (why?) livin' with you, then bein' spayed...or what they call neutered...is a pretty dog-gone important thing if you want to keep 'em healthy, and I'm sure you do.

Here's the deal with that there spaying. First of all, you don't get to eat or drink nuthin' all night long. I mean, what's up with

THAT? After supper, there's nuthin'! No snacks...no fried pig ears, no rawhide strips, no nuthin'! And then when breakfast time comes the next morning? Nuthin' again! Now, that didn't bother my sister Belle too much, 'cause she was too busy snorin'. But I was, like, starvin' to death! Then the Mister tells us it's time to go for a ride...which is music to a Lab's ears... especially when we thought we was goin' to a parade...and me and Belle went runnin' lickety-split and jumped right up in the Mister's car, ready to roll. But did we go downtown to watch a parade? No. Did we go to the park to chase squirrels? Nope. Did we even get to go to the pet store to be bathed and brushed? Heck no. We went to the veterinarian!

Now...let me tell you somethin' about that there vet. OK, I'll admit that she makes me and my sister feel good when we started out feelin' puny. And she's a good tummy scratcher, too. But like I've told you before in this here book, she can pull what you call a thermometer out of NOWHERE and stick it SOMEWHERE until that sucker completely disappears...which should be against the law in Texas and I just think it might be. And evidently part of that there spaying process involves not only takin' your temperature like you're checkin' the oil, but makin' you feel so sleepy that all you want to do is take a nap...which is pretty natural for a Lab, now that I think about it. Well, the next thing both me and my sister know, we're wakin'

up and each of us have a dad-gum satellite dish around our head. Why, I don't know. But wearing that big plastic collar keeps you from scratchin' and lickin' and even seein' what's comin' up behind you. And a Lab that can't scratch or lick or see where it's been is pretty useless. So what do Belle and I do? We go right back to sleep...which again is pretty natural for us...and the next time we wake up we're HOME. And we don't even remember how we got there. We don't remember goin' or comin'...but the bottom line is, we're HOME. Neither of us have any idea what happened, but I sure do know this about that: if anyone tells you you're goin' to a parade, run for the hills!

But be sure to grab yourself a fried pig ear before you go.

Doing What We Do Best

Well, I hope you enjoyed reading this here book. I know me and Chloe (OK...and the Mister, too) enjoyed puttin' these stories together for you. In fact...if the truth be known...it was the Missus' idea all along. For years she'd been trying to talk the Mister into writin' a book, but he kept sayin' he just couldn't come up with the right subject. And then me and my insane little sister came on the scene, and the rest is publishin' history, so to speak. So I guess you could say that we wrote this here best seller for the Missus. I mean, after all, if it wasn't for her, who would let us sleep inside on the couch all night long? Or all morning long? Or all afternoon long? Or who would make sure we had dozens of peanut butter-filled dog bones

stored in a box out in the garage? And who would give us one every time we looked hungry and pitiful (even if the Mister had just fed us)? Or who would give us a rawhide stick pretty near every time we begged for one? Not the Mister, that's for dog-gone sure.

Yep, me and my sister got the Missus wrapped around our paws...and she wouldn't have it any other way.

Now, just because this here book is finished don't mean me and Chloe are through sneakin' out and havin' a personal one-on-one with the Mister's brisket the next chance we get, or that we've given up chasin' squirrels or that we're gonna quit causing neighbor Bill's cat so much stress that his hair falls out like he's plannin' on makin' a cat-hair carpet or something. Nope. We're just done with this here book, that's all. For the time being, anyway. Why, to tell the truth, me and my sister have a whole bunch of new stories, just waitin' to be told. As soon as the Mister finds out about 'em, that is.

Like a few days ago when our spastic little yapper cousins, Coconut and Molly, came over for a visit. I was stretched out on the couch eatin' a fried pig ear when that little nut-case Molly snuck over and stood up on her hind feet along the side of the couch. I snuck a quick look-see and you know what I saw? Two beady little eyes just starin' at that pig ear. Why, she was like some kind of rat terrier giraffe, just stretchin'

and stretchin', standin' on her toenails tryin' to make herself tall enough to see what I was up to. I'm minding my own business now, and out of the corner of my eye I watch that little heathen terrier quietly tip-toe over and try to take my pig ear OUT OF MY MOUTH! Now, I've seen her do some strange things before, but I swear she must have a death wish, and I decided right then and there to try to oblige her. I let her have both barrels of one of my barks, and that little rat hound went into one of her catatonic trances...I mean, she just froze up stiff as a board, looked straight up at the ceiling, and then fell right over backwards with all four paws sticking up in the air. And you want to know what happened next?

That'll be in our next book.

Afterword: Why the Mister Wrote This Book

Now here's the deal: the Mister done wrote all these stories about me and my sister Chloe in order to help the Missus when she had what her doctor called a "mild stroke" (it might have been mild to him, but it sure wasn't to us). Anyway, it seems the doc told the Missus that she should read as much as possible, to exercise her thinkin' skills, whatever that means. All I know is she liked readin' stories about me and Chloe so much, that the Mister kept writin' them and he finally put 'em all in this here book. And evidently it worked, because the Missus done got feelin' fine and dandy. And now it seems like pretty near everyone is readin' this here book...and that includes YOU, and it evidently included the President of these here United States of America as well as his lovely wife, the Missus Bush. I guess you could say that me and my sister are now what you could call Dog-gone Celebrities!

Laura Bush

March 20, 2009

Mr. Doyle Walker
4421 Birdsong Lane
Plano, Texas 75093

Dear Mr. Walker,

Thank you for your nice letter and the inscribed copy of your book, *The Misadventures of Belle and Chloe*.

The publication of your short stories is a great tribute to your commitment to helping your wife recover from a stroke. I admire you for writing about your chocolate labs' antics to help her "exercise her brain" and overcome the challenges she faced following the stroke. That she has since regained her math skills is a wonderful testament to your role in her recovery!

Belle and Chloe are terrific characters, and I can understand why children enjoy reading about them. To help a child discover the joy of reading is one of the greatest gifts you can give.

President Bush joins me in sending our best wishes for Cathy's continued good health – and for the success of your book!

With warm regards,

Laura Bush

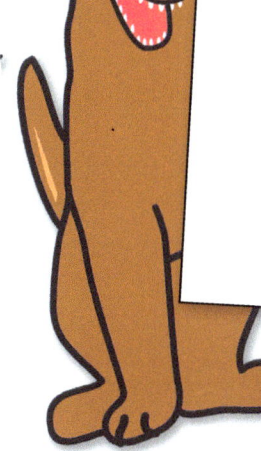

Index

A-B
C-D
E-F
G-H
I-J-K
L-M
N-O
P-Q
R-S
T

The one about the BBQ Brisket... 62
The one about the Bassinette 73
The one about Begging.. 48
The one about Belle's Lump 22
The one about CPR for Dogs.. 41
The one about Christmas Lights...................................... 65
The one about the Door-to-Door Preachers 44
The one about the Ducks.. 15
The one about Molly and Coconut................................... 19
The one about Molly and the Pig Ear 83
The one about Mouth-to-Snout Resuscitation..................... 35
The one about Naming the Pups 1
The one about the Parade 79
The one about Pinky 70
The one about the Possum 25
The one about the President and Mrs. Bush 86
The one about Rusty and the Rat 8
The one about the Squirrel in the Den.............................. 30
The one about the Squirrel in the Flowerbed...................... 53
The one about the Top Ten List 59
The one about Walking the Dogs...................................... 4

U-V
W-X
Y-Z

The Misadventures of Belle & Chloe

Belle, the Mister, and Chloe

The Misadventures of Belle & Chloe

The Misadventures of Belle & Chloe

www.ingramcontent.com/pod-product-compliance
Lightning Source LLC
Chambersburg PA
CBHW041512220426
43661CB00047B/1538